Matplotlib

In 8 Hours

For Beginners

Learn Coding Fast

Ray Yao

About the Authors: Ray Yao's Team

Certified PHP engineer by Zend, USA

Certified JAVA programmer by Sun, USA

Certified SCWCD developer by Oracle, USA

Certified A+ professional by CompTIA, USA

Certified ASP. NET expert by Microsoft, USA

Certified MCP professional by Microsoft, USA

Certified TECHNOLOGY specialist by Microsoft, USA

Certified NETWORK+ professional by CompTIA, USA

www.amazon.com/author/ray-yao

About This Book

"Matplotlib in 8 Hours" is a textbook for high school and college students; it covers all essential Matplotlib language knowledge. You can learn complete primary skills of Matplotlib programming fast and easily.

The textbook includes a lot of practical examples for beginners and includes exercises for the college final exam, the engineer certification exam, and the job interview exam.

"Matplotlib in 8 Hours" is a useful textbook for beginners. The straightforward definitions, the plain examples, the elaborate explanations and the neat layout feature this helpful and educative book. You will be impressed by its distinctive and tidy writing style. Reading this book is a great enjoyment!

Note

This book is only suitable for Matplotlib programming beginners, high school students and college students; it is not for the experienced Matplotlib programmers.

Prerequisite to Learn Matplotlib

Before learning the Matplotlib, you should have basic knowledge of Python.

(Each Cheat Sheet contains more than 300 examples, more than 300 outputs, and more than 300 explanations.)

Table of Contents

Matplotlib Q & A......................113

Recommended Books by Ray Yao........126

Hour 1

Prerequisite to Learn Matplotlib

Before learning the Matplotlib, you should have basic knowledge of Python.

What is Matplotlib Language?

Matplotlib is probably the most widely used suite on the Python 2D-drawing field, which makes it easy for users to graph data and provides a variety of output formats.

The feature of the Matplotlib is as follows:

1. Matplotlib is a primary Python graphic drawing library that is used as a visualization tool.

2. Matplotlib was invented by John Hunter.

3. Matplotlib is completely open source and can be used freely.

4. Matplotlib is composed primarily in Python language.

5. Matplotlib is compatible with C and JavaScript.

6. Matplotlib runs on Python platform.

Install Matplotlib

1. Before installing Matplotlib, you need to install the latest version Python to your local computer. The Python download link is:

https://www.python.org/

2. Having downloaded the Python installer, you can install Python.

3. After installing Python, please restart your computer.

4. Test the Python. Please click:

Window System > Command Prompt > Input the following command:

C:\User\YourName>python

5. If you can see the Python version, it means that Python have installed successfully.

6. The command to install Matplotlib is:

C:\User\YourName>pip install matplotlib

7. Please click:

Window System > Command Prompt > Input the following command:

C:\User\YourName>pip install matplotlib

```
C:\Users\RAY>pip install matplotlib
```

8. After installing Matplotlib, you can see:

```
C:\Users\RAY>pip install matplotlib
Requirement already satisfied: matplotlib
site-packages (3.4.1)
Requirement already satisfied: numpy>=1.1
\site-packages (from matplotlib) (1.20.2)
Requirement already satisfied: kiwisolver
39\lib\site-packages (from matplotlib) (1
Requirement already satisfied: pyparsing>
9\lib\site-packages (from matplotlib) (2.
Requirement already satisfied: cycler>=0.
b\site-packages (from matplotlib) (0.10.0
Requirement already satisfied: pillow>=6.
ib\site-packages (from matplotlib) (8.2.0
Requirement already satisfied: python-dat
hon39\lib\site-packages (from matplotlib)
```

9. Congratulation! Matplotlib has been installed successfully!

Set Up Python Editor

We need to set up Python first so that it can work as a Matplotlib editor.

1. Please click:

Python3.9 > IDLE (Python 3.9 64-bit) > open the Python editor.

2. Please click:

Options > Configure IDLE > General > Open Edit Window > OK.

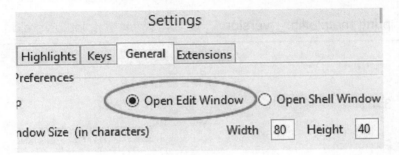

3. Restart the Python/Matplotlib Editor.

Congratulation! You can easily edit your Matplotlib program by using this editor from now on.

Import Matplotlib

We need to import Matplotlib library before doing something with Matplotlib programming.

The syntax to import Matplotlib library is:

```
import matplotlib
```

Example 1.1

```
import matplotlib
print( matplotlib.__version__ )     # check Matplotlib version
```

Output:

3.4.3

Explanation:

"**import matplotlib**" is used to import the Matplotlib library.

"matplotlib.__version__" checks the Matplotlib version.

"3.4.3" is the version of Matplotlib library.

Pyplot & NumPy

Pyplot is a sub module of Matplotlib, which is used to draw graphs. Usually Pyplot is given an alias "plt". When drawing a graph, we need to import Pyplot first.

NumPy is a Python library. It is used to work with arrays.

The syntax to import a Pyplot and NumPy is:

```
import matplotlib.pyplot as plt
import numpy as np
```

"plt" is the alias of Pyplot. "np" is the alias of NumPy.

Example 1.2

Draw a line from position (0, 0) to position (5, 200)

```
import matplotlib.pyplot as plt
import numpy as np
x = np.array([0, 5])
y = np.array([0, 200])
plt.plot(x, y)
plt.show()
```

Output:

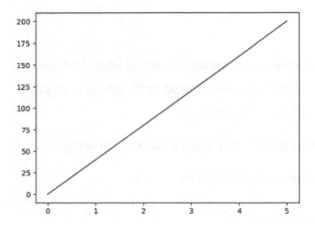

Explanation:

"import matplotlib.pyplot as plt" imports Pyplot and give it an alias "plt". Pyplot is a sub module of Matplotlib, which is used to draw graphs.

"import numpy as np" imports Numpy and give it an alias "np". NumPy is a Python library, which is used to work with arrays.

"x = np.array([0, 5])" & " y = np.array([0, 200])" defines a line from 0 to 5 on x-axis and from 0 to 200 on y-axis.

"plt.plot(x, y)" draws a line based on x and y.

"plt.show()" shows the graph.

Start Point & End Point

Drawing a line needs a starting point and an ending point.

The syntax to represent a starting point and an ending point is:

```
x = np.array([start, end])

y = np.array([start, end])
```

"x" represents the starting point and the ending point on x-axis.

"y" represents the starting point and the ending point on y-axis.

For Example

"**x = np.array([1, 10])**" represents that the line's starting point is 1, the ending point is 10 on x-axis.

"**y = np.array([3, 30])**" represents that the line's starting point is 3, the ending point is 30 on y-axis.

Plotting

"plot()" is used to draw a graph based on the parameters.

The syntax of plot() is:

```
plot(x, y)
```

Parameter x represents the starting point and the ending point on the x-axis.

Parameter y represents the starting point and the ending point on the y-axis.

Example 1.3

```
import matplotlib.pyplot as plt
import numpy as np
x = np.array([2, 9])
y = np.array([5, 12])
plt.plot(x, y)
plt.show()
```

Output:

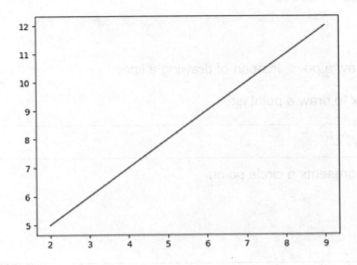

Explanation:

" **plt.plot(x, y)**" draws a graph based on the parameters x and y.

"x = np.array([2, 9])" represents the starting point 2 and the ending point 9 on the x-axis.

"y = np.array([5, 12])" represents the starting point 5 and the ending point 12 on the y-axis.

Draw a Point

We can draw a point, instead of drawing a line.

The syntax to draw a point is:

```
plt.plot(x, y, 'o')
```

'o' letter represents a circle point.

Example 1.4

```
import matplotlib.pyplot as plt

import numpy as np

x = np.array([ 2 ])

y = np.array([ 5 ])

plt.plot(x, y, 'o')

plt.show()
```

Output:

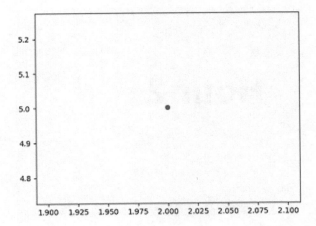

Explanation:

"plt.plot(x, y, 'o')" uses a parameter 'o', which makes to draw a point only, instead of drawing a line.

'o' letter represents the circle point.

Note:

If the code is "x = np.array([**x1, x2, x3, ...**])   y = np.array([**y1, y2, y3, ...**])", the "plt.plot(x, y, 'o')" will draw multiple circle points.

Hour 2

Draw a Curve

We can draw a curve by using multiple points.

The syntax to define multiple points is:

```
x = np.array([x1, x2, x3, x4])
y = np.array([y1, y2, y3, y4])
```

"x" defines multiple points on x-axis.

"y" defines multiple points on y-axis.

Example 2.1

```
import matplotlib.pyplot as plt
import numpy as np
x = np.array([2, 4, 8, 9])
y = np.array([10, 60, 30, 80])
plt.plot(x, y)
plt.show()
```

Output:

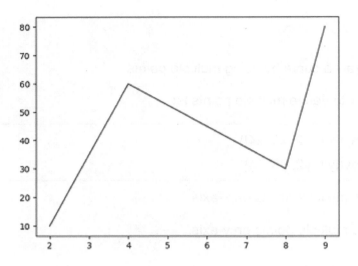

Explanation:

"x = np.array([2, 4, 8, 9])" defines four points (2,4,8,9) on x-axis.

"y = np.array([10, 60, 30, 80])" defines four points (10, 60, 30, 80) on y-axis.

"plt.plot(x, y)" draws a curve based on the (2,4,8,9) on x-axis and the (10, 60, 30, 80) on y-axis.

Default Points on x-axis

Sometimes, if we only define the points on y-axis and do not define the points on x-axis, the default points on x-axis are (0, 1, 2, 3, 4, 5) just like this:

```
x = np.array([0, 1, 2, 3, 4, 5])
```

Example 2.2

```
import matplotlib.pyplot as plt

import numpy as np

y = np.array([2, 7, 5, 8, 3, 9])

plt.plot(y)

plt.show()
```

Output:

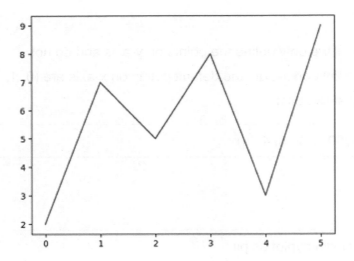

Explanation:

"y = np.array([2, 7, 5, 8, 3, 9])" defines the points on y-axis.

Note: this program has not defined the points on x-axis, so the default points on x-axis are (0, 1, 2, 3, 4, 5).

Marker

We can set up each point presented by a specified symbol.

For example: we can present each point with star symbol, diamond symbol, or circle symbol……

The syntax to set up a symbol to present a point is:

plot(y, marker = 'symbol')

Example 2.3

```
import matplotlib.pyplot as plt

import numpy as np

y = np.array([2, 7, 5, 8, 3, 9])

plt.plot(y, marker = '*')     # set up a star symbol

plt.show()
```

Output:

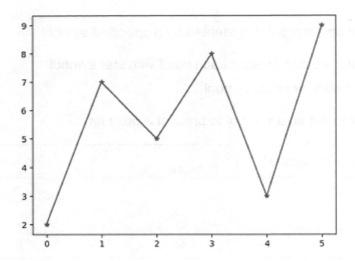

Explanation:

"plt.plot(y, marker = '*')" sets up each point presented by the star symbol.

So we can see that each point is a star symbol.

Marker Symbols

Matplotlib provides following Marker Symbols for developers.

Marker	Represent
'*'	star
'o'	circle
','	pixel
'.'	point
'X'	X
'x'	x (small)
'P'	Plus
'+'	plus (small)
'D'	Diamond
'd'	diamond (small)
's'	square
'p'	pentagon
'H'	Hexagon
'h'	hexagon (small)
'^'	up triangle
'v'	down triangle
'>'	right triangle
'<'	left triangle
'|'	vertical line
'_'	horizon line

The following is an example, we set up the marker to a circle symbol by using 'o'.

```
plot(y, marker = 'o')
```

Note: the 'o' is not a zero, it is an English letter.

Example 2.4

```
import matplotlib.pyplot as plt

import numpy as np

y = np.array([2, 7, 5, 8, 3, 9])

plt.plot(y, marker = 'o')      # set up a circle symbol

plt.show()
```

Output:

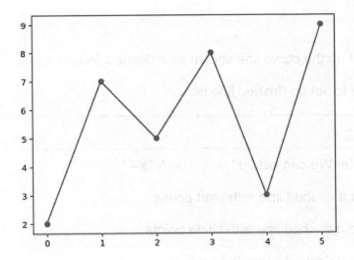

Explanation:

"plt.plot(y, marker = 'o')" sets up each point presented by the circle symbol.

So we can see that each point is a circle symbol.

Dashed Line

We can set up the curve line shown as a dashed line.

The syntax to set up dashed line is:

```
' symbol -- '
```

For example: We can set up ' *-- ', ' o-- ', ' x-- '

'*--' sets up a dashed line with start points

'o--' sets up a dashed line with circle points

'x--' sets up a dashed line with 'x' points

Example 2.5

```python
import matplotlib.pyplot as plt

import numpy as np

y = np.array([2, 7, 5, 8, 3, 9])

plt.plot(y, 'x--')     # set up a dashed line with 'x' points

plt.show()
```

Output:

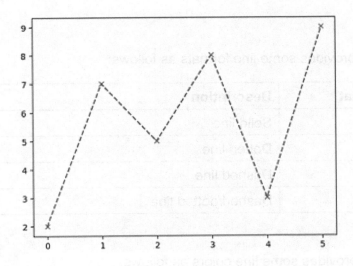

Explanation:

"plt.plot(y, 'x--')" sets up the curve shown as a dashed line with 'x' points.

Line Format & Color

Matplotlib provides some line formats as follows:

Line Format	Description
'-'	Solid line
':'	Dotted line
'--'	Dashed line
'-.'	Dashed/dotted line

Matplotlib provides some line colors as follows:

Color	Description
'r'	Red
'g'	Green
'b'	Blue
'c'	Cyan
'm'	Magenta
'y'	Yellow
'k'	Black
'w'	White

We will study the line format and color in the next chapter.

Hour 3

Line Color

In the last chapter, we know that the 'r' represents red, 'y' represents yellow, 'g' represents green......

Now we can set the line color by using 'r', 'y', 'g'......

The syntax to set the color of a line is:

'marker format color'

Example 3.1

```
import matplotlib.pyplot as plt

import numpy as np

y = np.array([2, 9, 3, 8])

plt.plot(y, 'd-.r')

plt.show()
```

Output:

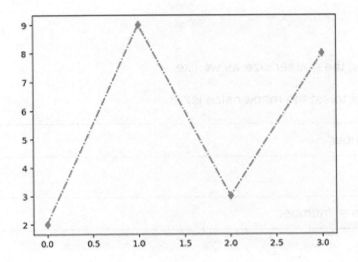

Explanation:

"plt.plot(y, 'd-.r')" sets the marker to 'd', sets the format to '-.',
sets the color to 'r'.

'd' represents a diamond.

'-.' represents a dashed/dotted line.

'r' represents red.

Marker Size

We can set the marker size as we like.

The syntax to set the marker size is:

```
ms =  'number'
```

or

```
markersize =  'number'
```

Example 3.2

```
import matplotlib.pyplot as plt

import numpy as np

y = np.array([2, 9, 3, 8])

plt.plot(y, marker = '*', ms = '18')

plt.show()
```

Output:

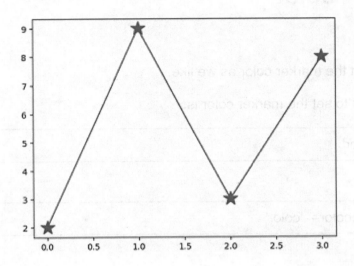

Explanation:

"ms = '18'" sets the markersize to 18.

We can alternatively use "markersize = '18'" to set the marker size.

Marker Color

We can set the marker color as we like.

The syntax to set the marker color is:

mfc = 'color'

or

markerfacecolor= 'color'

Example 3.3

```
import matplotlib.pyplot as plt

import numpy as np

y = np.array([2, 9, 3, 8])

plt.plot(y, marker = '*', ms = 18, mfc = 'r')

plt.show()
```

Output:

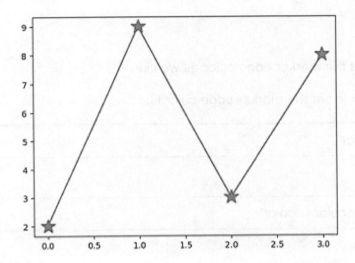

Explanation:

" **mfc = 'r'**" sets the marker color to red.

We can alternatively use "markerfacecolor = 'r'" to set the marker color to red.

Marker Edge Color

We can set the marker edge color as we like.

The syntax to set the marker edge color is:

```
mec =  'color'
```

or

```
markeredgecolor=  'color'
```

Example 3.4

```
import matplotlib.pyplot as plt

import numpy as np

y = np.array([2, 9, 3, 8])

plt.plot(y, marker = 'o', ms = 18, mfc = 'b', mec = 'r')

plt.show()
```

Output:

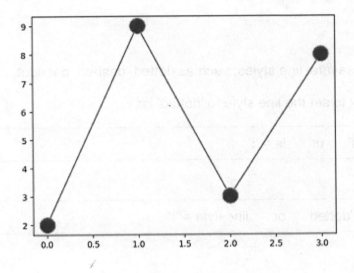

Explanation:

" **mec = 'r'**" sets the marker edge color to red.

We can alternatively use "markeredgecolor = 'r'" to set the marker edge color to red.

Dotted Line Style

There are several line styles, such as dotted, dashed, dashdot...

The syntax to set the line style to 'dotted' is:

ls = 'dotted'   or   ls = ':'

or

linestyle = 'dotted'   or   linestyle = ':'

Example 3.5

```
import matplotlib.pyplot as plt

import numpy as np

y = np.array([2, 9, 3, 8])

plt.plot(y, ls = 'dotted')    # ls = ':'

plt.show()
```

Output:

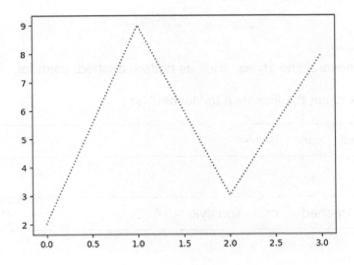

Explanation:

"plt.plot(y, ls = 'dotted')" sets the line style to dotted.

We can alternatively use **'linestyle = 'dotted'** to set the line style to dotted. The other line styles of Matplotlib are:

Style	Symbol
'solid' (default)	'-'
'dotted'	':'
'dashed'	'--'
'dashdot'	'-.'

Dashed Line Style

There are several line styles, such as dotted, dashed, dashdot...

The syntax to set the line style to 'dashed' is:

ls = 'dashed'   or   ls = '--'

or

linestyle = 'dashed'   or   linestyle = '--'

Example 3.6

```
import matplotlib.pyplot as plt

import numpy as np

y = np.array([2, 9, 3, 8])

plt.plot(y, ls = 'dashed')     # ls = '--'

plt.show()
```

Output:

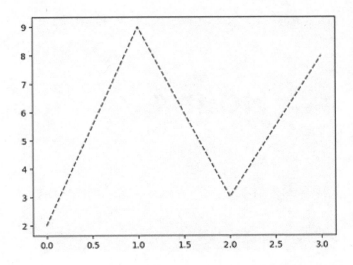

Explanation:

"plt.plot(y, ls = 'dashed')" sets the line style to dashed.

We can alternatively use **'linestyle = 'dashed'** to set the line style to dashed.

There is another lined style called 'dashdot' or '-.'

(We can try another line style 'dashdot' or '-.'

Please set **ls = 'dashdot'**, and study the output result.)

Hour 4

Line Color

We can set the color of the line.

The syntax to set the line color is:

c = 'color'

or

color = 'color'

Example 4.1

```
import matplotlib.pyplot as plt
import numpy as np
y = np.array([2, 9, 3, 8])
plt.plot(y, ls = 'dashdot', color = 'r')     # c='r'
plt.show()
```

Output:

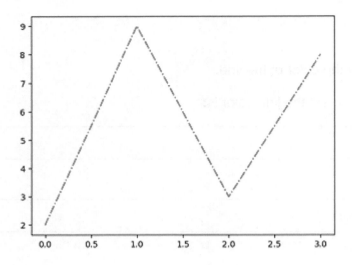

Explanation:

"ls = 'dashdot'" sets the line style to dashed/dotted.

"color = 'r'" sets the line color to red.

"c = 'r'" sets the line color to red.

Line Width

We can set the width of the line.

The syntax to set the line width is:

lw = 'number'

or

linewidth = 'number'

Example 4.2

```
import matplotlib.pyplot as plt

import numpy as np

y = np.array([2, 9, 3, 8])

plt.plot(y, ls = 'dashdot', linewidth = '10')    # lw = '18'

plt.show()
```

Output:

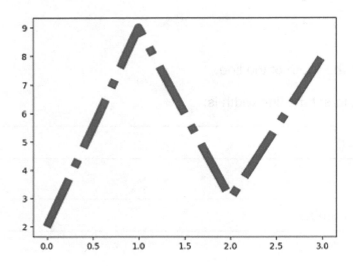

Explanation:

"ls = 'dashdot'" sets the line style to dashed/dotted.

"linewidth = '10'" sets the line width to 10.

"lw = '10'" sets the line width to 10.

Two Curves

We can draw two curves simultaneously.

The syntax to define two curves is:

```
# define curve1
x1 = np.array([...])
y1 = np.array([...])
# define curve 2
x2 = np.array([...])
y2 = np.array([...])
```

Example 4.3

```
import matplotlib.pyplot as plt
import numpy as np
x1 = np.array([1, 4, 6, 7])
y1 = np.array([1, 5, 3, 9])
x2 = np.array([0, 3, 4, 7])
y2 = np.array([0, 7, 1, 8])
plt.plot(x1, y1, x2, y2)     # draw two curves
plt.show()
```

Output

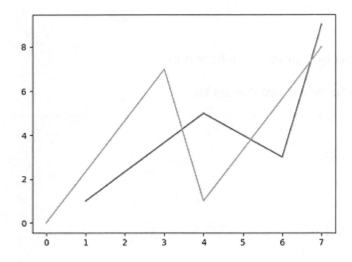

Explanation:

x1 = np.array([1, 4, 6, 7]) and **y1 = np.array([1, 5, 3, 9])** defines the blue curves.

x2 = np.array([0, 3, 4, 7]) and **y2 = np.array([0, 7, 1, 8])** defines the yellow curves.

"plt.plot(x1, y1, x2, y2)" draws two curves simultaneously.

We can draw multiple curves by using the above method.

Matplotlib Labels

We can set a label to the x-axis and y-axis respectively.

The syntax to set the labels to x-axis and y-axis is:

```
plt.xlabel("label-name")
plt.ylabel("label-name")
```

Example 4.4

```
import numpy as np

import matplotlib.pyplot as plt

x = np.array([1, 2, 3, 4, 5, 6])

y = np.array([100, 200, 300, 400, 500, 600])

plt.plot(x, y)

plt.xlabel("Hours")

plt.ylabel("Miles")

plt.show()
```

Output:

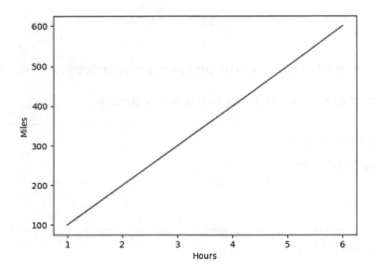

Explanation:

"plt.xlabel("Hours")" sets the label name of the x-axis to Hours.

"plt.ylabel("Miles")" sets the label name of the y-axis to Miles.

Matplotlib Title

We can set a title for the chart.

The syntax to set a title for the chart is:

```
plt.title("title")
```

Example 4.5

```
import numpy as np

import matplotlib.pyplot as plt

x = np.array([1, 2, 3, 4, 5, 6])

y = np.array([100, 200, 300, 400, 500, 600])

plt.plot(x, y)

plt.title("Speed Chart")

plt.xlabel("Hours")

plt.ylabel("Miles")

plt.show()
```

Output:

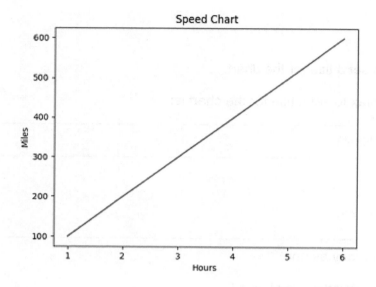

Explanation:

"plt.title("Speed Chart")" sets the title to "Speed Chart".

We can see the "Speed Chart" on the top of the chart.

Set the Font

We can set the font of the title and labels.

The syntax to set the font is:

```
fontdict = font
```

Example 4.6

```
import numpy as np
import matplotlib.pyplot as plt
x = np.array([1, 2, 3, 4, 5, 6])
y = np.array([100, 200, 300, 400, 500, 600])
plt.plot(x, y)
font1 = {'family':'DejaVu Sans','color':'red','size':28}
font2 = {'family':'DejaVu Sans','color':'blue','size':18}
font3 = {'family':'DejaVu Sans','color':'green','size':18}
plt.title("Speed Chart", fontdict = font1)
plt.xlabel("Hours", fontdict = font2)
plt.ylabel("Miles", fontdict = font3)
plt.show()
```

Output:

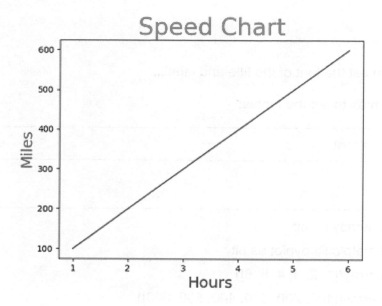

Explanation:

"fontdict = font1" sets the font1's property.

"fontdict = font2" sets the font2's property.

"fontdict = font3" sets the font3's property.

Hour 5

Align the Title

The syntax to align the title is:

loc = 'left / center / right'

The default position of the title is 'center'.

Example 5.1

```
import numpy as np

import matplotlib.pyplot as plt

x = np.array([1, 2, 3, 4, 5, 6])

y = np.array([100, 200, 300, 400, 500, 600])

plt.plot(x, y)

plt.title("Speed Chart", loc = 'right')

plt.xlabel("Hours")

plt.ylabel("Miles")

plt.show()
```

Output:

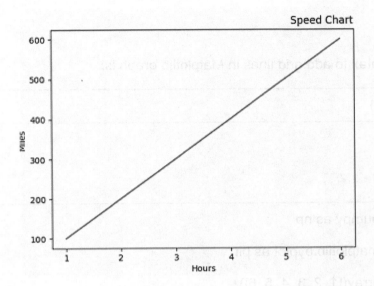

Explanation:

"Loc = 'right'" sets the title to align to the right.

We can see the title "Speed Chart" on the right top corner.

Matplotlib Grid Lines

The syntax to add grid lines in Matplotlib graph is:

```
plt.grid()
```

Example 5.2

```
import numpy as np

import matplotlib.pyplot as plt

x = np.array([1, 2, 3, 4, 5, 6])

y = np.array([100, 200, 300, 400, 500, 600])

plt.plot(x, y)

plt.title("Speed Chart")

plt.xlabel("Hours")

plt.ylabel("Miles")

plt.grid()

plt.show()
```

Output:

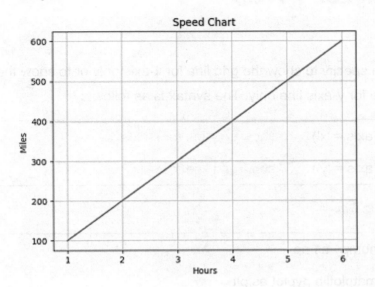

Explanation:

"plt.grid()" adds grid lines in the Matplotlib graph.

X-Axis or Y-Axis

We can specify to show the grid line for x-axis only or to show the grid line for y-axis line only. The syntax is as follows:

```
plt.grid(axis = 'x')     # show grid line for x-axis

plt.grid(axis = 'y')     # show grid line for y-axis
```

Example 5.3

```
import numpy as np

import matplotlib.pyplot as plt

x = np.array([1, 2, 3, 4, 5, 6])

y = np.array([100, 200, 300, 400, 500, 600])

plt.plot(x, y)

plt.title("Speed Chart")

plt.xlabel("Hours")

plt.ylabel("Miles")

plt.grid(axis = 'x')     # show grid line for x-axis

plt.show()
```

Output:

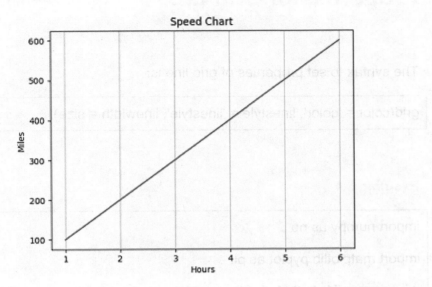

Explanation:

"plt.grid(axis = 'x')" shows the grid line for x-axis.

Properties of Grid Line

The syntax to set properties of grid line is:

grid(color = 'color', linestyle = 'linestyle', linewidth = size)

Example 5.4

```
import numpy as np

import matplotlib.pyplot as plt

x = np.array([1, 2, 3, 4, 5, 6])

y = np.array([100, 200, 300, 400, 500, 600])

plt.plot(x, y)

plt.title("Speed Chart")

plt.xlabel("Hours")

plt.ylabel("Miles")

plt.grid(color = 'red', linestyle = '-.', linewidth = 1.2)

plt.show()
```

Output:

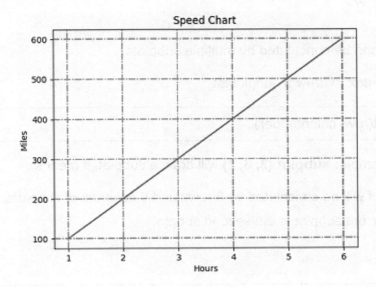

Explanation:

"plt.grid(color = 'red', linestyle = '-.', linewidth = 1.2)" sets the property of the grid line. Therefore, we can see the result:

The color of the grid line is red.

The style of the grid line is dash dot.

The width of the grid line is 1.2

Multiple Subplots

A plot can be constituted by multiple subplots.

The syntax to draw a subplot is:

```
subplot(row, col, number)
```

For example: **subplot (3, 6, 2)** will draw a subplot, it means:

The plot will be constituted by 3 rows and 6 columns of subplots. The current subplot is the second subplot.

Example 5.5

```
import matplotlib.pyplot as plt
import numpy as np
y = np.array([1, 6, 5, 6])    # define the first subplot
plt.subplot(1, 2, 1)
plt.plot(y)
y = np.array([2, 9, 3, 8])    # define the second subplot
plt.subplot(1, 2, 2)
plt.plot(y)
plt.show()
```

Output:

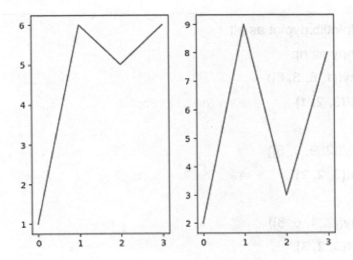

Explanation:

The above plot is constituted by two subplots.

"subplot(1, 2, 1)" will draw a subplot, it means that there is 1 row, 2 columns of subplots in the whole plot. The current subplot is the first plot.

"subplot(1, 2, 2)" will draw a subplot, it means that there is 1 row, 2 columns of subplots in the whole plot. The current subplot is the second plot.

Example 5.6

```
import matplotlib.pyplot as plt
import numpy as np
y = np.array([1, 6, 5, 6])
plt.subplot(3, 2, 1)     # draw the 1st subplot
plt.plot(y)
y = np.array([2, 9, 3, 8])
plt.subplot(3, 2, 2)     # draw the 2nd subplot
plt.plot(y)
y = np.array([2, 4, 6, 8])
plt.subplot(3, 2, 3)     # draw the 3rd subplot
plt.plot(y)
y = np.array([8, 6, 4, 2])
plt.subplot(3, 2, 4)     # draw the 4th subplot
plt.plot(y)
y = np.array([8, 3, 9, 2])
plt.subplot(3, 2, 5)     # draw the 5th subplot
plt.plot(y)
y = np.array([6, 5, 6, 1])
plt.subplot(3, 2, 6)     # draw the 6th subplot
plt.plot(y)
plt.show()
```

Output:

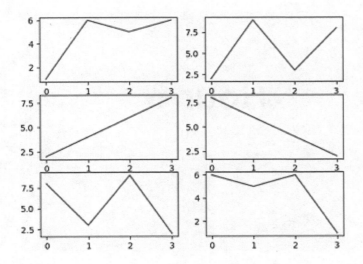

Explanation:

The whole plot is constituted by total 3 rows and 2 columns of subplots.

Hour 6

Title of the Subplot

The syntax to set a super title of all subplots is:

suptitle("title")

The syntax to set a subtitle of each subplot is:

title("subtitle")

Example 6.1

```
import matplotlib.pyplot as plt
import numpy as np
y = np.array([1, 6, 5, 6])
plt.subplot(1, 2, 1)
plt.plot(y)
plt.title("The 1st Plot")
y = np.array([2, 9, 3, 8])
plt.subplot(1, 2, 2)
plt.plot(y)
plt.title("The 2nd Plot")
plt.suptitle("Super Plot")
plt.show()
```

Output:

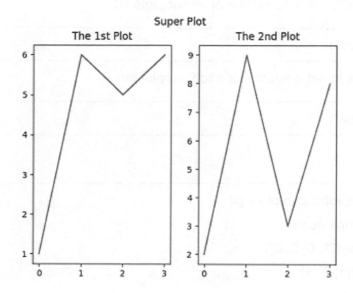

Explanation:

"plt.suptitle("Super Plot")" sets a super title of the whole figure.

"plt.title("The 1st Plot")" sets a subtitle for the first plot.

"plt.title("The 2nd Plot")" sets a subtitle for the second plot.

Scatter Plots

Scatter Plots can help to analyze the relationship between x points and y points. For example, most of the products own such trend: the higher price, the fewer sales. Otherwise, the lower price, the more sale. The syntax to define scatter plots is:

```
plt.scatter(x, y)
```

In the following example, the x-axis represents the 'price', the y-axis represents the 'sale'.

Example 6.2

```
import matplotlib.pyplot as plt
import numpy as np
x = np.array([15,5,9,3,13,7,20])
y = np.array([16,68,32,80,23,52,10])
plt.scatter(x, y)
plt.show()
```

Output:

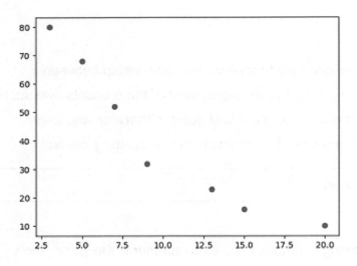

Explanation:

"plt.scatter(x, y)" sets up the scatter plots.

In the above example, the x-axis represents the 'price', the y-axis represents the 'sale'.

From the scatter plot, it seems that the higher price, the fewer sale; the lower price, the more sale.

More Scatter Plots

In order to confirm the relationships between x points and y points, we can draw two scatter plots in the same figure.

Example 6.3

```
import matplotlib.pyplot as plt

import numpy as np

x = np.array([15,5,9,3,13,7,20,])

y = np.array([16,68,32,80,23,52,10])

plt.scatter(x, y)

x = np.array([16,3,12,8,18,5,19,])

y = np.array([18,76,30,48,14,61,9])

plt.scatter(x, y)

plt.show()
```

Output:

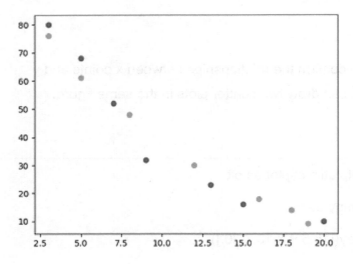

Explanation:

The blue points come from the first scatter plots.

The yellow points come from the second plots.

From the above figure, we find that two scatter plots own the same trend. Therefore, we can confirm the conclusion:

The higher the price, the less the sales. Otherwise, the lower price, the more sale.

Color of Scatter Plots

The syntax to set the color of the scatter plots is:

```
color = 'color'    or    c = 'color'
```

Example 6.4

```
import matplotlib.pyplot as plt

import numpy as np

x = np.array([15,5,9,3,13,7,20,])

y = np.array([16,68,32,80,23,52,10])

plt.scatter(x, y, c = 'red')

x = np.array([16,3,12,8,18,5,19,])

y = np.array([18,76,30,48,14,61,9])

plt.scatter(x, y, c = 'green')

plt.show()
```

Output:

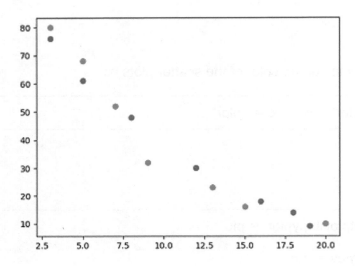

Explanation:

c = 'red' sets the first plot to red.

c = 'green' sets the second plot to green.

Color of Each Point

The syntax to set different color of each point is:

c = colors

Example 6.5

```
import matplotlib.pyplot as plt

import numpy as np

x = np.array([15,5,9,3,13,7,20])

y = np.array([16,68,32,80,23,52,10])

myColors =
np.array(["green","red","orange","pink","gray","blue","cyan"])

plt.scatter(x, y, c=myColors)

plt.show()
```

Output:

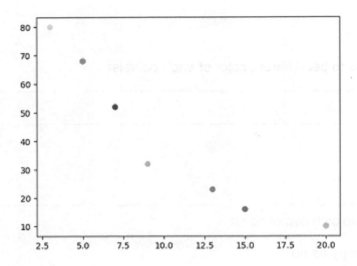

Explanation:

"myColors = np.array(["green","red","orange","pink","gray","blue","cyan"])" creates an array to include different colors.

NumPy is a Python library.

"np.array()" is a Numpy statement, which is used for working with Python arrays.

"c=myColors" sets the different color of each point.

Size & Alpha

The syntax to set the size of the points is:

s = size   # usually size range is from 1 to 1000

The syntax to set the alpha of the points is:

alpha = number   # transparence range is from 0 to 1

Example 6.6

```
import matplotlib.pyplot as plt

import numpy as np

x = np.array([15,5,9,3,13,7,20])

y = np.array([16,68,32,80,23,52,10])

myColors =
np.array(["green","red","orange","pink","gray","blue","cyan"])

plt.scatter(x, y, s = 200, alpha = 0.4)

plt.show()
```

Output

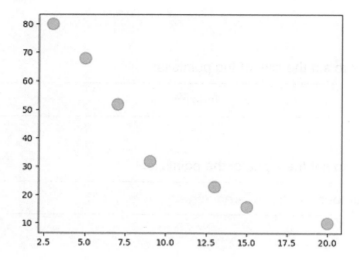

Explanation:

" **s = 200** " sets the size of the points.

The larger size value, the bigger size.

" **alpha = 0.4** " sets the transparency of the point.

The larger alpha value, the more transparent.

Hour 7

Matplotlib Bars

We can draw some bars in a figure.

The syntax to set up to draw bars is:

```
bar(x,y)
```

"x" can be presented by "A, B, C, ..." or "one, two, three, ...", which actually are the names of the bars.

Example 7.1

```
import matplotlib.pyplot as plt

import numpy as np

x = np.array(["1st", "2nd", "3rd", "4th", "5th"])

y = np.array([5, 9, 3, 8, 6])

plt.bar(x,y)

plt.show()
```

Output:

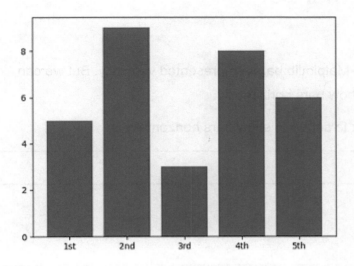

Explanation:

"plt.bar(x,y)" sets up to draw some bars in the figure.

"x = np.array(["1st", "2nd", "3rd", "4th", "5th"])" defines the names of the five bars.

Horizontal Bar

By default, Matplotlib bars are presented vertically. But we can set up to show bars horizontally.

The syntax to set up to show bars horizontally is:

```
barh(x, y)
```

Example 7.2

```
import matplotlib.pyplot as plt
import numpy as np
x = np.array(["1st", "2nd", "3rd", "4th", "5th"])
y = np.array([5, 9, 3, 8, 6])
plt.barh(x,y)
plt.show()
```

Output:

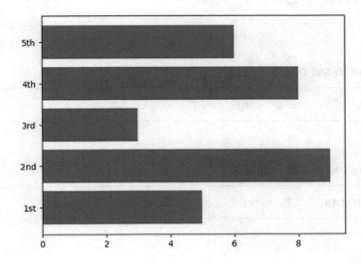

Explanation:

"**plt.barh(x,y)**" sets up to show the bars horizontally.

Bar Color, Bar Width

The syntax to set bar color is:

```
color = "color"    # color value can be a color name or hex
```

The syntax to set bar width is:

```
width = number    # bar width is used for vertical bars only
```

Example 7.3

```
import matplotlib.pyplot as plt

import numpy as np

x = np.array(["1st", "2nd", "3rd", "4th", "5th"])

y = np.array([5, 9, 3, 8, 6])

plt.bar(x, y, color = "red", width = 0.5)

plt.show()
```

Output:

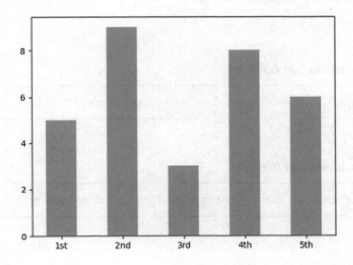

Explanation:

"color = "red"" sets the bar color to red.

"width = 0.5" sets the bar width to 0.5.

Bar Color, Bar Height

The syntax to set bar color is:

color = "color"   # color value can be a color name or hex

The syntax to set bar width is:

height = number   # bar height is used for horizontal bars only

Example 7.4

```
import matplotlib.pyplot as plt

import numpy as np

x = np.array(["1st", "2nd", "3rd", "4th", "5th"])

y = np.array([5, 9, 3, 8, 6])

plt.barh(x, y, color = "#339900", height = 0.4)

plt.show()
```

Output:

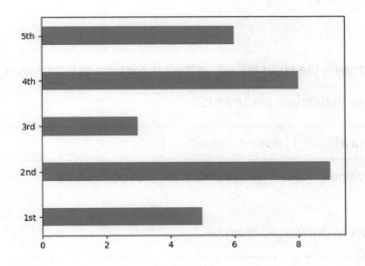

Explanation:

"color = "#339900"" sets the bar color to green.

"height = 0.4" sets the bar height to 0.4.

Pie Chart

We can draw a pie chart based on the percentage of each value.

The syntax to define a pie chart is:

```
y = np.array([value1, value2, value3, …])
```

"value1, value2, value3" is the percentage of each value.

The syntax to draw a pie chart is:

```
plt.pie(y)
```

Example 7.5

```
import matplotlib.pyplot as plt

import numpy as np

y = np.array([60, 30, 10])

plt.pie(y)

plt.show()
```

Output:

Explanation:

In the above figure, we can see that the blue value is 60%, the orange value is 30%, the green value is 10%.

By default, the plotting of the pie chart starts from the x-axis, and rotates counterclockwise.

One piece of the pie chart is called "wedge".

Label of Pie Chart

The syntax to define the labels of each wedge is:

```
labels = wedge_names
```

Example 7.6

```
import matplotlib.pyplot as plt

import numpy as np

y = np.array([40, 30, 10, 20])     # percentage

myPets = ["cat", "dog", "fox", "owl"]

plt.pie(y, labels = myPets)

plt.show()
```

Output:

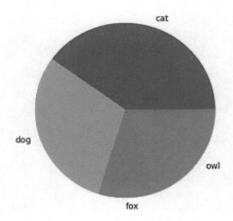

Explanation:

According to the above example, Cat is 40%, Dog is 30%, Fox is 10%, and Owl is 20%.

"myPets = ["cat", "dog", "fox", "owl"]" sets myPets including four kinds of pets.

"labels = myPets" defines the labels of each kind of pets.

Hour 8

Start Angle

Be default, the rotation of the pie chart starts from 0 degree. But we can set the rotation to start at any Angle.

The syntax to set the start angle is:

```
startangle =  degree
```

Example 8.1

```
import matplotlib.pyplot as plt

import numpy as np

y = np.array([40, 30, 10, 20])

myPets = ["cat", "dog", "fox", "owl"]

plt.pie(y, labels = myPets, startangle = 180)

plt.show()
```

Output

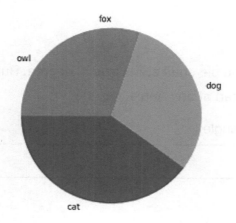

Explanation:

"startangle = 180" sets the rotation to start at 180 degrees, and rotates counterclockwise.

Pie Chart Explode

If we want one of the wedges to stand out, we can set this wedge slightly away from the center.

The syntax to set a standout wedge is:

```
standout = [ v1, v2, v3, v4]

explode = standout
```

For example: if v1 is set 0.3, but v2, v3, v4 is set 0, then the wedge corresponding to the v1 will stand out.

Example 8.2

```
import matplotlib.pyplot as plt

import numpy as np

y = np.array([40, 30, 10, 20])

myPets = ["cat", "dog", "fox", "owl"]

standout = [0, 0.1, 0, 0]    # the v2 is set 0.1

plt.pie(y, labels = myPets, explode = standout)

plt.show()
```

Output:

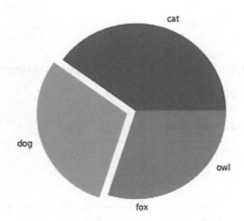

Explanation:

In the above example: v1 is corresponding cat, v2 is corresponding dog, v3 is corresponding fox, v4 is corresponding owl.

"standout = [0, 0.1, 0, 0]" sets v2 to 0.1, but the rest is 0, so the wedge corresponding to the 0.1 is a standout wedge.

Note: "v1, v2, v4" is set 0, which means the wedge corresponding to 'v1, v2, v4' do not stand out.

Pie Chart Shadow

We can add a shadow to the pie chart.

The syntax to add a shadow to a pie chart is:

```
shadow = True
```

Example 8.3

```
import matplotlib.pyplot as plt

import numpy as np

y = np.array([40, 30, 10, 20])

myPets = ["cat", "dog", "fox", "owl"]

standout = [0, 0.1, 0, 0]     # the v2 is set 0.1

plt.pie(y, labels = myPets, explode = standout, shadow = True)

plt.show()
```

Output:

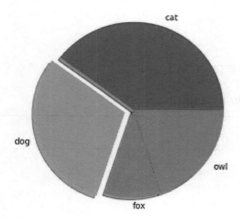

Explanation:

" **shadow = True** " adds a shadow to the pie chart.

Pie Chart Color

The syntax to add colors to a pie chart is:

```
colors = [ "color1", "color2", "color3",......]
```

Example 8.4

```
import matplotlib.pyplot as plt

import numpy as np

y = np.array([40, 30, 10, 20])

myPets = ["cat", "dog", "fox", "owl"]

standout = [0, 0.1, 0, 0]     # the v2 is set 0.1

plt.pie(y, labels = myPets, explode = standout,

colors = ["red", "g", "b", "#000000"])

plt.show()
```

Output:

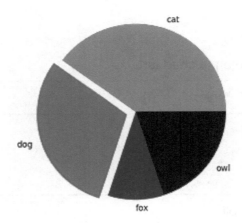

Explanation:

In the above example, 'color1' is corresponding cat, 'color2' is corresponding dog, 'color3' is corresponding fox, 'color4' is corresponding owl.

"colors = ["red", "g", "b", "#000000"])" sets cat to red, sets dog to green, sets fox to blue, and sets owl to black.

'r'	red	'm'	magenta
'g'	green	'y'	yellow
'b'	blue	'k'	black
'c'	cyan	'w'	white

Pie Chart Legend

We can add an illustration to a pie chart.

The syntax to add an illustration to a pie chart is:

```
plt.legend()
```

Example 8.5

```
import matplotlib.pyplot as plt

import numpy as np

y = np.array([40, 30, 10, 20])

myPets = ["cat", "dog", "fox", "owl"]

plt.pie(y, labels = myPets)

plt.legend()

plt.show()
```

Output:

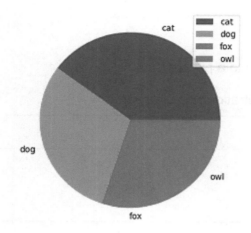

Explanation:

"plt.legend()" adds an illustration to the pie chart.

The illustration in Matplotlib is called "legend".

Legend with Title

We can add a title to a legend.

The syntax to add a title to a legend is:

```
title = "myTitle"
```

Example 8.6

```
import matplotlib.pyplot as plt

import numpy as np

y = np.array([40, 30, 10, 20])

myPets = ["cat", "dog", "fox", "owl"]

plt.pie(y, labels = myPets)

plt.legend(title = "Our Pets:")

plt.show()
```

Output:

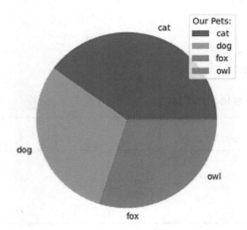

Explanation:

"**plt.legend(title = "Our Pets:")**" adds a title to the pie chart, the title is "Our Pets:".

Matplotlib
Q & A

Questions

Please fill in the correct answers:

01.

import matplotlib.pyplot as <u>fill in</u>   # alias

import numpy as np

x = np.array([0, 5])

y = np.array([0, 200])

plt.plot(x, y)

plt.show()

A. pyplot   B. py   C. plot   D. plt

02.

import matplotlib.pyplot as plt

import numpy as np

x = np.<u>fill in</u>([2, 4, 8, 9])

y = np.<u>fill in</u>([10, 60, 30, 80])

"x" defines multiple points in x-axis.

"y" defines multiple points in y-axis.

A. matplotlib   B. pyplot   C. array   D. numpy

03.

```
import matplotlib.pyplot as plt
import numpy as np
y = np.array([2, 9, 3, 8])
plt.plot(y, fill in r')   # set a diamond, dashdot line
plt.show()
```

A. diamond-.   B. d-.   C. diamond..   D. d..

04.

```
import matplotlib.pyplot as plt
import numpy as np
y = np.array([2, 9, 3, 8])
plt.plot(y, ls = 'dashdot', fill in = 'r')     # set up the color
plt.show()
```

A. a   B. b   C. c   D. d

05.

```
x = np.array([1, 2, 3, 4, 5, 6])
y = np.array([100, 200, 300, 400, 500, 600])
plt.plot(x, y)
```

115

```
plt.title("Speed Chart", fill in = 'right')   # align the title

plt.xlabel("Hours")

plt.ylabel("Miles")

plt.show()
```

A. loc   B. align   C. location   D. position

06.

```
y = np.array([1, 6, 5, 6])

plt.subplot(1, 2, 1)

plt.plot(y)

plt.title("The 1st Plot")

y = np.array([2, 9, 3, 8])

plt.subplot(1, 2, 2)

plt.plot(y)

plt.title("The 2nd Plot")

plt.fill in("Super Plot")   # set a supper title

plt.show()
```

A. supper   B. title   C. supertitle   D. suptitle

07.

```
x = np.array(["1st", "2nd", "3rd", "4th", "5th"])
```

```python
y = np.array([5, 9, 3, 8, 6])

plt.fill in(x,y)    # set up to draw a bar

plt.show()
```

A. draw   B. bar   C. drawbar   D. bars

08.

```python
import matplotlib.pyplot as plt

import numpy as np

y = np.array([40, 30, 10, 20])

myPets = ["cat", "dog", "fox", "owl"]

plt.pie(y, labels = myPets, fill in = 180)
# set up a start angle

plt.show()
```

A. startangle   B. start_angle   C. start   D. angle

09.

```python
import matplotlib.pyplot as plt

import numpy as np

x = np.array([2, 9])

y = np.array([5, 12])

plt.fill in(x, y)    # draw a graph based on the x and y
```

plt.show()

A. draw   B. paint   C. fecit   D. plot

10.

Marker	Represent
'*'	star
'o'	circle
'H'	Hexagon
'h'	hexagon (small)
'X'	X
'x'	x (small)
'P'	Plus
'p'	fill in

A. plus(small)   B. letter 'p'   C. pentagon   D. purple

11.

import matplotlib.pyplot as plt

import numpy as np

y = np.array([2, 9, 3, 8])

plt.plot(y, marker = '*', ms = 18, <u>fill in</u> = 'r')

set up the marker color

plt.show()

A. markercolor   B. mfc   C. color   D. mc

12.

```
import matplotlib.pyplot as plt

import numpy as np

y = np.array([2, 9, 3, 8])

plt.plot(y, ls = 'dashdot', fill in = '10')

# set up the line width

plt.show()
```

A. linewidth   B. widthOfLine   C. width   D. w

13.

```
x = np.array([1, 2, 3, 4, 5, 6])

y = np.array([100, 200, 300, 400, 500, 600])

plt.plot(x, y)

plt.title("Speed Chart")

plt.xlabel("Hours")

plt.ylabel("Miles")

plt.fill in()     # adds grid lines in the graph

plt.show()
```

A. grid   B. gridline   C. lattice   D. net

14.

```
import matplotlib.pyplot as plt
import numpy as np
x = np.array([15,5,9,3,13,7,20])
y = np.array([16,68,32,80,23,52,10])
plt.fill in(x, y)    # set up scatter plots
plt.show()
```

A. scatterplots   B. scatterplot   C. scatter   D. plots

15.

```
import matplotlib.pyplot as plt
import numpy as np
y = np.array([60, 30, 10])
plt.fill in(y)    # set up a pie chart
plt.show()
```

A. piechart   B. pieChart   C. pie_chart   D. pie

16.

```
y = np.array([40, 30, 10, 20])
myPets = ["cat", "dog", "fox", "owl"]
```

120

```
plt.pie(y, labels = myPets)

plt.fill in()     # add an illustration to the pie chart

plt.show()
```

A. add   B. illustration   C. legend   D. figure

17.
```
import matplotlib.pyplot as plt

import numpy as np

x = np.array([ 2 ])

y = np.array([ 5 ])

plt.plot(x, y, 'fill in')     # set to draw a circle point

plt.show()
```
A. circle   B. o   C. point   D. p

18.
```
import matplotlib.pyplot as plt

import numpy as np

y = np.array([2, 7, 5, 8, 3, 9])

plt.plot(y, 'fill in')     # set a dashed line with 'x' points

plt.show()
```

A. x-   B. x: C. x-.   D. x--

121

19.

```python
import matplotlib.pyplot as plt
import numpy as np
y = np.array([2, 9, 3, 8])
plt.plot(y, ls = 'fill in')    # set up a dotted line style
plt.show()
```

A. -   B. :   C. -.   D. --

20.

```python
x = np.array([1, 2, 3, 4, 5, 6])
y = np.array([100, 200, 300, 400, 500, 600])
plt.plot(x, y)
font1 = {'family':'DejaVu Sans','color':'red','size':28}
font2 = {'family':'DejaVu Sans','color':'blue','size':18}
font3 = {'family':'DejaVu Sans','color':'green','size':18}
plt.title("Speed Chart", fill in = font1)    # set a font
plt.xlabel("Hours", fill in = font2)    # set a font
plt.ylabel("Miles", fill in = font3)    # set a font
plt.show()
```

A. font   B. fontAttribute   C. fontdict   D. fontProperty

21.

```
y = np.array([1, 6, 5, 6])

plt.fill in(1, 2, 1)    # draw the first subplot

plt.plot(y)

y = np.array([2, 9, 3, 8])

plt.fill in(1, 2, 2)    # draw the second subplot

plt.plot(y)

plt.show()
```

A. subplot   B. subplots   C. drawsubplot   D. sub

22.

```
x = np.array([15,5,9,3,13,7,20])

y = np.array([16,68,32,80,23,52,10])

myColors =
np.array(["green","red","orange","pink","gray","blue","cyan"])

plt.scatter(x, y, s = 200, alpha = fill in)   # set up the alpha

plt.show()
```

A. -0.5   B. 0.5   C. 1.5   D. 2.5

23.

```
x = np.array(["1st", "2nd", "3rd", "4th", "5th"])

y = np.array([5, 9, 3, 8, 6])

plt.fill in(x,y)     # set up a horizontal bar

plt.show()
```

A. horizontalbar   B.hbar   C. barh   D. barhorizontal

24.

```
y = np.array([40, 30, 10, 20])

myPets = ["cat", "dog", "fox", "owl"]

standout = [0, 0.1, 0, 0]     # the v2 is set 0.1

plt.pie(y, labels = myPets, fill in = standout)

# set a wedge slight standout

plt.show()
```

A. wedge   B. pie   C. piechart   D. explode

Answers

01. D	09. D	17. B
02. C	10. C	18. D
03. B	11. B	19. B
04. C	12. A	20. C
05. A	13. A	21. A
06. D	14. C	22. B
07. B	15. D	23. C
08. A	16. C	24. D

Recommended Books by Ray Yao

(Each Cheat Sheet contains more than 300 examples, more than 300 outputs, and more than 300 explanations.)

Paperback Books by Ray Yao

C# Cheat Sheet

C++ Cheat Sheet

Java Cheat Sheet

JavaScript Cheat Sheet

Php MySql Cheat Sheet

Python Cheat Sheet

Html Css Cheat Sheet

Linux Command Line

C# 100 Q & A

C++ 100 Q & A

Java 100 Q & A

JavaScript 100 Q & A

Php MySql 100 Q & A

Python 100 Q & A

Html Css 100 Q & A

Linux 100 Q & A

C# Examples

C++ Examples

Java Examples

JavaScript Examples

Php MySql Examples

Python Examples

Html Css Examples

Shell Scriptng Examples

Advanced C++ in 8 hours

Advanced Java in 8 hours

AngularJs in 8 hours

C# programming

C++ programming

Dart in 8 hours

Django in 8 hours

Erlang in 8 hours

Git Github in 8 hours

Golang in 8 hours

Google Sheets in 8 hours

Haskell in 8 hours

Html Css programming

Java programming

JavaScript programming

JQuery programming
Kotlin in 8 hours
Lua in 8 hours
Matlab in 8 hours
Matplotlib in 8 hours
MySql database
Node.Js in 8 hours
NumPy in 8 hours
Pandas in 8 hours
Perl in 8 hours
Php MySql programming
PowerShell in 8 hours
Python programming
R programming
React.Js in 8 hours
Ruby programming
Rust in 8 hours
Scala in 8 hours
Shell Scripting in 8 hours
Swift in 8 hours
TypeScript in 8 hours
Visual Basic programming
Vue.Js in 8 hours
Xml Json in 8 hours

Made in United States
Troutdale, OR
12/30/2024

27434901R00073